The Egg Lover's Cookbook: 50 Ways to Enjoy Eggs

By: Kelly Johnson

Table of Contents

- Classic Scrambled Eggs
- Fluffy Omelet
- Soft-Boiled Eggs with Soldiers
- Perfect Hard-Boiled Eggs
- Deviled Eggs
- Classic Eggs Benedict
- Poached Eggs with Avocado Toast
- Spanish Tortilla
- Shakshuka (Poached Eggs in Spiced Tomato Sauce)
- Huevos Rancheros
- Egg Salad Sandwich
- Cloud Eggs
- Baked Eggs in Avocado
- Scotch Eggs
- Quiche Lorraine
- Spinach and Feta Frittata
- Croque Madame
- Egg Drop Soup
- Tamago Sushi (Japanese Omelet on Rice)
- Korean Gyeran Jjim (Steamed Eggs)
- Chinese Tea Eggs
- Thai Son-in-Law Eggs
- Egg Curry
- Classic French Soufflé
- Pasta Carbonara
- Egg Fried Rice
- Egg-Stuffed Peppers
- Breakfast Burrito with Eggs
- Turkish Cilbir (Poached Eggs with Yogurt)
- Cheesy Baked Egg Casserole
- Eggs in Purgatory (Spicy Tomato Sauce)
- Baked Egg and Cheese Cups
- Mushroom and Swiss Omelet
- Breakfast Tacos with Scrambled Eggs
- Japanese Omurice (Omelet over Fried Rice)

- Classic French Toast
- Chawanmushi (Japanese Savory Egg Custard)
- Egg Foo Young (Chinese Omelet)
- Keto Egg Muffins
- Smoked Salmon and Egg Bagel
- Baked Eggplant Parmesan with Egg
- Pesto and Parmesan Baked Eggs
- Egg-Stuffed Meatloaf
- Eggnog
- Chocolate Lava Cake with Eggs
- Lemon Curd (Egg-Based)
- Vanilla Custard
- Tiramisu (Egg-Based Dessert)
- Crème Brûlée
- Meringue Cookies

Classic Scrambled Eggs

Ingredients:

- 4 large eggs
- ¼ cup whole milk (optional, for creaminess)
- Salt, to taste
- Black pepper, to taste
- 1 tbsp butter

Instructions:

1. **Whisk the eggs** – In a bowl, beat the eggs with milk (if using), salt, and pepper until well combined.
2. **Heat the pan** – Place a nonstick skillet over medium-low heat and melt the butter.
3. **Cook the eggs** – Pour the eggs into the pan and let them sit undisturbed for a few seconds.
4. **Gently stir** – Using a spatula, slowly stir and fold the eggs, pushing them from the edges toward the center.
5. **Remove from heat** – When the eggs are soft and slightly undercooked, remove from heat. The residual heat will finish cooking them.
6. **Serve immediately** – Enjoy warm with toast, herbs, or cheese if desired.

Fluffy Omelet

Ingredients:

- 3 large eggs
- 2 tbsp milk or water
- Salt, to taste
- Black pepper, to taste
- 1 tbsp butter
- ¼ cup shredded cheese (optional)
- Fresh herbs or fillings of choice (optional)

Instructions:

1. **Whisk the eggs** – In a bowl, beat the eggs with milk or water, salt, and pepper until frothy.
2. **Heat the pan** – Melt butter in a nonstick skillet over medium-low heat.
3. **Cook the eggs** – Pour the eggs into the pan and let them cook undisturbed for a few seconds.
4. **Lift and tilt** – Gently lift the edges with a spatula, tilting the pan to let uncooked egg flow underneath.
5. **Add fillings (if using)** – Sprinkle cheese or other fillings over one side.
6. **Fold and serve** – Once the omelet is set but still slightly soft in the center, fold it in half and slide it onto a plate. Serve immediately.

Soft-Boiled Eggs with Soldiers

Ingredients:

- 2 large eggs
- Water, for boiling
- Salt and pepper, to taste
- 2 slices of toasted bread, cut into strips

Instructions:

1. **Boil water** – Bring a saucepan of water to a gentle boil.
2. **Cook the eggs** – Lower the eggs into the water and simmer for 6 minutes for a runny yolk.
3. **Cool slightly** – Remove eggs and place in cold water for 30 seconds.
4. **Crack and serve** – Tap the top of the eggs with a spoon and remove the shell.
5. **Dip and enjoy** – Serve with toast strips for dipping.

Perfect Hard-Boiled Eggs

Ingredients:

- 4 large eggs
- Water, for boiling
- Ice water, for cooling

Instructions:

1. **Boil water** – Fill a pot with enough water to cover the eggs and bring to a rolling boil.
2. **Cook the eggs** – Gently lower the eggs into the water and boil for 10–12 minutes.
3. **Cool immediately** – Transfer eggs to an ice bath and let them sit for at least 5 minutes.
4. **Peel and serve** – Gently crack the shell and peel under running water for easy removal.

Deviled Eggs

Ingredients:

- 6 large eggs, hard-boiled and peeled
- 3 tbsp mayonnaise
- 1 tsp Dijon mustard
- ½ tsp white vinegar
- Salt and pepper, to taste
- Paprika, for garnish
- Chopped chives or parsley (optional)

Instructions:

1. **Halve the eggs** – Cut the eggs in half lengthwise and remove the yolks.
2. **Make the filling** – Mash the yolks with mayonnaise, mustard, vinegar, salt, and pepper until smooth.
3. **Fill the eggs** – Spoon or pipe the mixture back into the egg whites.
4. **Garnish and serve** – Sprinkle with paprika and herbs if using.

Classic Eggs Benedict

Ingredients:

- 2 English muffins, split and toasted
- 4 large eggs
- 4 slices of Canadian bacon
- 1 tbsp white vinegar
- ½ cup hollandaise sauce (homemade or store-bought)
- Chopped chives (optional)

Instructions:

1. **Poach the eggs** – Bring water to a simmer with vinegar and gently add eggs, cooking for 3–4 minutes.
2. **Cook the bacon** – In a skillet, lightly brown the Canadian bacon.
3. **Assemble** – Place bacon on toasted muffin halves, top with poached eggs, and drizzle with hollandaise sauce.
4. **Garnish and serve** – Sprinkle with chives if desired.

Poached Eggs with Avocado Toast

Ingredients:

- 2 slices of bread, toasted
- 1 ripe avocado, mashed
- 2 large eggs
- 1 tbsp white vinegar
- Salt, pepper, and red pepper flakes (to taste)
- Olive oil (optional)

Instructions:

1. **Poach the eggs** – Simmer water with vinegar, swirl, and cook eggs for 3–4 minutes.
2. **Prepare toast** – Spread mashed avocado on toast and season.
3. **Top with eggs** – Gently place poached eggs on top and drizzle with olive oil.

Spanish Tortilla

Ingredients:

- 4 large eggs
- 2 medium potatoes, thinly sliced
- ½ onion, thinly sliced
- 3 tbsp olive oil
- Salt and pepper, to taste

Instructions:

1. **Cook potatoes and onions** – Sauté in olive oil over medium heat until tender.
2. **Mix with eggs** – In a bowl, whisk eggs and combine with cooked potatoes.
3. **Cook tortilla** – Pour mixture into the pan, cook until set, then flip and cook the other side.

Shakshuka (Poached Eggs in Spiced Tomato Sauce)

Ingredients:

- 4 large eggs
- 1 can (14 oz) crushed tomatoes
- 1 small onion, diced
- 2 garlic cloves, minced
- 1 tsp cumin
- ½ tsp paprika
- Salt and pepper, to taste
- 1 tbsp olive oil
- Chopped cilantro (optional)

Instructions:

1. **Sauté onion and garlic** – Cook in olive oil until softened.
2. **Add spices and tomatoes** – Stir in cumin, paprika, salt, and pepper. Simmer for 10 minutes.
3. **Poach the eggs** – Make small wells in the sauce, crack in eggs, cover, and cook until set.

Huevos Rancheros

Ingredients:

- 2 large eggs
- 2 corn tortillas
- ½ cup refried beans
- ½ cup salsa
- ¼ cup crumbled queso fresco
- 1 tbsp olive oil

Instructions:

1. **Fry tortillas** – Heat in a pan until crisp.
2. **Cook eggs** – Fry eggs to preferred doneness.
3. **Assemble** – Spread beans on tortillas, top with eggs, salsa, and cheese.

Egg Salad Sandwich

Ingredients:

- 4 hard-boiled eggs, chopped
- ¼ cup mayonnaise
- 1 tsp Dijon mustard
- ½ tsp lemon juice
- Salt and pepper, to taste
- 4 slices of bread
- Lettuce (optional)

Instructions:

1. **Mix ingredients** – Combine eggs, mayo, mustard, lemon juice, salt, and pepper.
2. **Assemble sandwich** – Spread onto bread with lettuce if desired.

Cloud Eggs

Ingredients:

- 2 large eggs
- Salt and pepper, to taste
- 2 tbsp grated Parmesan (optional)

Instructions:

1. **Separate the eggs** – Whip egg whites to stiff peaks.
2. **Bake the whites** – Spoon onto a parchment-lined tray, making a small well in each.
3. **Add yolks** – Place yolks in the center and bake at 375°F (190°C) for 3–5 minutes.

Baked Eggs in Avocado

Ingredients:

- 1 ripe avocado, halved and pitted
- 2 small eggs
- Salt and pepper, to taste
- Red pepper flakes (optional)

Instructions:

1. **Preheat oven** – Set to 375°F (190°C).
2. **Prepare avocado** – Scoop out some flesh to fit eggs.
3. **Bake** – Crack an egg into each half and bake for 12–15 minutes.

Scotch Eggs

Ingredients:

- 4 large eggs, hard-boiled and peeled
- ½ lb ground sausage
- ½ cup all-purpose flour
- 1 egg, beaten
- 1 cup breadcrumbs
- Salt and pepper, to taste
- Oil for frying

Instructions:

1. **Wrap the eggs** – Flatten sausage and wrap each egg completely.
2. **Coat** – Roll in flour, dip in beaten egg, and coat with breadcrumbs.
3. **Fry** – Heat oil to 350°F (175°C) and fry until golden brown.

Quiche Lorraine

Ingredients:

- 1 pre-made pie crust
- 4 large eggs
- 1 cup heavy cream
- ½ cup cooked bacon, chopped
- ½ cup shredded Gruyère cheese
- Salt, pepper, and nutmeg (to taste)

Instructions:

1. **Preheat oven** – Set to 375°F (190°C).
2. **Prepare filling** – Whisk eggs, cream, and seasonings, then add bacon and cheese.
3. **Bake** – Pour into crust and bake for 35–40 minutes.

Spinach and Feta Frittata

Ingredients:

- 6 large eggs
- ½ cup crumbled feta
- 1 cup fresh spinach, chopped
- 1 tbsp olive oil
- Salt and pepper, to taste

Instructions:

1. **Preheat oven** – Set to 375°F (190°C).
2. **Sauté spinach** – Cook in a pan with olive oil until wilted.
3. **Mix and bake** – Whisk eggs, season, add feta and spinach, then bake for 15–20 minutes.

Croque Madame

Ingredients:

- 4 slices of bread
- 2 tbsp butter
- 2 tbsp Dijon mustard
- 4 slices ham
- ½ cup shredded Gruyère cheese
- 2 large eggs

Instructions:

1. **Assemble sandwich** – Spread mustard on bread, add ham and cheese.
2. **Toast** – Cook in buttered pan until golden.
3. **Top with egg** – Fry eggs and place one on each sandwich.

Egg Drop Soup

Ingredients:

- 4 cups chicken broth
- 2 large eggs, beaten
- 1 tbsp cornstarch mixed with 2 tbsp water
- Salt and white pepper, to taste
- 1 green onion, sliced

Instructions:

1. **Boil broth** – Heat until simmering.
2. **Thicken** – Stir in cornstarch mixture.
3. **Add eggs** – Slowly pour in eggs while stirring.
4. **Serve** – Season and garnish with green onions.

Tamago Sushi (Japanese Omelet on Rice)

Ingredients:

- 2 large eggs
- 1 tbsp sugar
- 1 tsp soy sauce
- 1 tsp mirin
- 1 cup sushi rice, cooked
- 1 sheet nori, cut into strips

Instructions:

1. **Cook tamago** – Whisk eggs with sugar, soy sauce, and mirin, then cook in a nonstick pan, folding into layers.
2. **Assemble sushi** – Shape rice, top with omelet, and wrap with nori.

Korean Gyeran Jjim (Steamed Eggs)

Ingredients:

- 3 large eggs
- ½ cup water or dashi
- ½ tsp salt
- 1 green onion, chopped

Instructions:

1. **Whisk eggs** – Mix with water and salt.
2. **Steam** – Cook in a heatproof bowl over simmering water for 10–12 minutes.
3. **Serve** – Garnish with green onions.

Chinese Tea Eggs

Ingredients:

- 6 large eggs, hard-boiled and cracked
- 2 cups water
- ½ cup soy sauce
- 2 black tea bags
- 1 cinnamon stick
- 2 star anise
- 1 tsp sugar

Instructions:

1. **Simmer marinade** – Combine all ingredients and simmer.
2. **Soak eggs** – Add cracked eggs and let steep for at least 4 hours or overnight.

Thai Son-in-Law Eggs

Ingredients:

- 4 large eggs, hard-boiled and peeled
- 2 tbsp fish sauce
- 1 tbsp palm sugar
- 1 tbsp tamarind paste
- 1 tbsp oil
- 2 shallots, fried
- Chili flakes and cilantro (for garnish)

Instructions:

1. **Fry eggs** – Deep-fry boiled eggs until golden.
2. **Make sauce** – Simmer fish sauce, sugar, and tamarind paste.
3. **Assemble** – Drizzle sauce over eggs and garnish.

Egg Curry

Ingredients:

- 4 hard-boiled eggs, peeled
- 1 onion, finely chopped
- 2 tomatoes, pureed
- 2 garlic cloves, minced
- 1-inch ginger, minced
- 1 tsp cumin
- 1 tsp coriander
- ½ tsp turmeric
- ½ tsp chili powder
- ½ cup coconut milk or water
- 2 tbsp oil
- Fresh cilantro for garnish

Instructions:

1. **Sauté onions, garlic, and ginger** – Cook in oil until soft.
2. **Add spices** – Stir in cumin, coriander, turmeric, and chili powder.
3. **Simmer sauce** – Add tomato puree and coconut milk, simmer for 10 minutes.
4. **Add eggs** – Gently add boiled eggs and cook for 5 minutes.
5. **Serve** – Garnish with cilantro.

Classic French Soufflé

Ingredients:

- 3 tbsp butter
- 3 tbsp flour
- 1 cup milk
- 4 large eggs, separated
- ½ tsp salt
- ½ cup grated Gruyère cheese

Instructions:

1. **Preheat oven** – Set to 375°F (190°C).
2. **Make roux** – Melt butter, stir in flour, and slowly add milk.
3. **Add yolks and cheese** – Stir into sauce and season.
4. **Whip egg whites** – Beat to stiff peaks, then fold into mixture.
5. **Bake** – Pour into buttered ramekins and bake for 25–30 minutes.

Pasta Carbonara

Ingredients:

- 8 oz spaghetti
- 2 large eggs
- ½ cup grated Parmesan
- 4 oz pancetta or bacon, diced
- Black pepper, to taste

Instructions:

1. **Cook pasta** – Boil until al dente and reserve ½ cup pasta water.
2. **Cook pancetta** – Fry until crispy.
3. **Mix eggs and cheese** – Whisk together.
4. **Combine** – Toss pasta with pancetta, remove from heat, then mix in egg mixture and reserved pasta water.
5. **Serve** – Garnish with black pepper and more Parmesan.

Egg Fried Rice

Ingredients:

- 2 cups cooked rice (day-old works best)
- 2 large eggs, beaten
- 1 carrot, diced
- ½ cup peas
- 2 green onions, chopped
- 2 tbsp soy sauce
- 1 tbsp oil

Instructions:

1. **Sauté vegetables** – Cook carrots and peas in oil.
2. **Scramble eggs** – Push veggies aside and cook eggs.
3. **Add rice** – Stir in rice, soy sauce, and green onions.

Egg-Stuffed Peppers

Ingredients:

- 2 bell peppers, halved and seeded
- 4 large eggs
- ½ cup shredded cheese
- Salt and pepper, to taste

Instructions:

1. **Preheat oven** – Set to 375°F (190°C).
2. **Fill peppers** – Crack an egg into each half, season, and top with cheese.
3. **Bake** – Cook for 15–20 minutes.

Breakfast Burrito with Eggs

Ingredients:

- 2 large eggs, scrambled
- 1 flour tortilla
- ¼ cup shredded cheese
- 2 tbsp salsa
- 2 tbsp cooked sausage or bacon
- ¼ avocado, sliced

Instructions:

1. **Scramble eggs** – Cook in a pan until fluffy.
2. **Assemble burrito** – Layer eggs, cheese, salsa, meat, and avocado on tortilla.
3. **Wrap and serve** – Fold and enjoy warm.

Turkish Çılbır (Poached Eggs with Yogurt)

Ingredients:

- 2 large eggs
- ½ cup Greek yogurt
- 1 garlic clove, minced
- 1 tbsp butter
- ½ tsp paprika
- 1 tbsp vinegar

Instructions:

1. **Poach eggs** – Cook in simmering water with vinegar.
2. **Prepare yogurt** – Mix yogurt with garlic and salt.
3. **Assemble** – Place poached eggs over yogurt, drizzle with melted butter and paprika.

Cheesy Baked Egg Casserole

Ingredients:

- 6 large eggs
- 1 cup milk
- 1 cup shredded cheese
- ½ cup diced bell peppers
- ½ cup cooked sausage or ham
- Salt and pepper, to taste

Instructions:

1. **Preheat oven** – Set to 375°F (190°C).
2. **Whisk eggs and milk** – Season and mix in cheese, peppers, and sausage.
3. **Bake** – Pour into greased dish and cook for 25 minutes.

Eggs in Purgatory (Spicy Tomato Sauce)

Ingredients:

- 4 large eggs
- 1 can (14 oz) crushed tomatoes
- 1 small onion, diced
- 2 garlic cloves, minced
- 1 tsp red pepper flakes
- 1 tbsp olive oil

Instructions:

1. **Sauté onion and garlic** – Cook in olive oil.
2. **Add tomatoes and spices** – Simmer for 10 minutes.
3. **Poach eggs** – Crack eggs into sauce, cover, and cook until set.

Baked Egg and Cheese Cups

Ingredients:

- 4 large eggs
- ½ cup shredded cheddar cheese
- 4 slices of ham or bacon (optional)
- Salt and pepper, to taste
- Chopped chives (optional)

Instructions:

1. **Preheat oven** – Set to 375°F (190°C).
2. **Prepare muffin tin** – Grease and line with ham or bacon if using.
3. **Assemble** – Crack an egg into each cup, season, and sprinkle with cheese.
4. **Bake** – Cook for 12–15 minutes until set.
5. **Serve** – Garnish with chives.

Mushroom and Swiss Omelet

Ingredients:

- 3 large eggs
- ½ cup sliced mushrooms
- ¼ cup shredded Swiss cheese
- 1 tbsp butter
- Salt and pepper, to taste

Instructions:

1. **Sauté mushrooms** – Cook in butter until tender.
2. **Whisk eggs** – Season and pour into pan.
3. **Cook omelet** – Let set, then add mushrooms and cheese.
4. **Fold and serve** – Cook until cheese melts.

Breakfast Tacos with Scrambled Eggs

Ingredients:

- 4 small tortillas
- 4 large eggs, scrambled
- ½ cup shredded cheese
- ½ cup cooked bacon or sausage
- Salsa and avocado (optional)

Instructions:

1. **Warm tortillas** – Heat in a dry pan.
2. **Assemble tacos** – Fill with scrambled eggs, cheese, and meat.
3. **Serve** – Top with salsa and avocado if desired.

Japanese Omurice (Omelet over Fried Rice)

Ingredients:

- 2 large eggs
- 1 cup cooked rice
- ¼ cup diced chicken or ham
- ¼ cup peas and carrots
- 2 tbsp ketchup
- 1 tbsp soy sauce
- 1 tbsp butter

Instructions:

1. **Prepare fried rice** – Sauté chicken, veggies, and rice in butter, adding ketchup and soy sauce.
2. **Make omelet** – Whisk eggs and cook in a pan until just set.
3. **Assemble** – Place omelet over rice and fold the edges.

Classic French Toast

Ingredients:

- 4 slices of bread
- 2 large eggs
- ½ cup milk
- 1 tbsp sugar
- ½ tsp cinnamon
- 1 tsp vanilla extract
- Butter for cooking

Instructions:

1. **Whisk batter** – Mix eggs, milk, sugar, cinnamon, and vanilla.
2. **Dip bread** – Soak each slice in the mixture.
3. **Cook** – Fry in butter until golden brown.
4. **Serve** – Top with syrup or fruit.

Chawanmushi (Japanese Savory Egg Custard)

Ingredients:

- 2 large eggs
- 1 cup dashi broth
- 1 tsp soy sauce
- 1 tsp mirin
- ¼ cup mushrooms, shrimp, or chicken (optional)

Instructions:

1. **Whisk eggs** – Mix with dashi, soy sauce, and mirin.
2. **Strain mixture** – Pour into cups with mushrooms or shrimp.
3. **Steam** – Cook over simmering water for 15 minutes.

Egg Foo Young (Chinese Omelet)

Ingredients:

- 4 large eggs
- ½ cup bean sprouts
- ¼ cup sliced mushrooms
- ¼ cup cooked shrimp or chicken
- 1 tbsp soy sauce

Instructions:

1. **Mix ingredients** – Beat eggs and combine with veggies and protein.
2. **Cook omelet** – Fry in a pan until golden.
3. **Serve** – Drizzle with soy sauce.

Keto Egg Muffins

Ingredients:

- 6 large eggs
- ½ cup shredded cheese
- ¼ cup diced bell peppers
- ¼ cup cooked bacon or sausage
- Salt and pepper, to taste

Instructions:

1. **Preheat oven** – Set to 375°F (190°C).
2. **Whisk eggs** – Mix with cheese, peppers, and meat.
3. **Bake** – Pour into greased muffin tins and cook for 15–20 minutes.

Smoked Salmon and Egg Bagel

Ingredients:

- 1 bagel, halved and toasted
- 2 large eggs, scrambled
- 2 oz smoked salmon
- 2 tbsp cream cheese
- Capers and dill (optional)

Instructions:

1. **Prepare bagel** – Spread cream cheese on each half.
2. **Assemble** – Layer scrambled eggs and salmon.
3. **Garnish** – Add capers and dill if desired.

Baked Eggplant Parmesan with Egg

Ingredients:

- 1 eggplant, sliced
- 2 large eggs, beaten
- ½ cup breadcrumbs
- 1 cup marinara sauce
- ½ cup shredded mozzarella
- ¼ cup Parmesan cheese

Instructions:

1. **Preheat oven** – Set to 375°F (190°C).
2. **Bread eggplant** – Dip slices in egg, then coat with breadcrumbs.
3. **Bake** – Cook for 20 minutes, then top with sauce and cheese.
4. **Finish** – Bake until cheese melts.

Pesto and Parmesan Baked Eggs

Ingredients:

- 4 large eggs
- 2 tbsp pesto
- ¼ cup grated Parmesan cheese
- Salt and pepper, to taste
- Fresh basil for garnish (optional)

Instructions:

1. **Preheat oven** – Set to 375°F (190°C).
2. **Prepare baking dish** – Grease a baking dish and spoon pesto into the bottom.
3. **Add eggs** – Crack eggs over pesto and season with salt and pepper.
4. **Bake** – Sprinkle with Parmesan and bake for 12–15 minutes, until eggs are set.
5. **Serve** – Garnish with basil and serve warm.

Egg-Stuffed Meatloaf

Ingredients:

- 1 lb ground beef
- 1 onion, diced
- 1 egg (for filling)
- 1 cup breadcrumbs
- 1 tsp garlic powder
- 1 tsp Worcestershire sauce
- 2 hard-boiled eggs
- Salt and pepper, to taste

Instructions:

1. **Preheat oven** – Set to 350°F (175°C).
2. **Prepare filling** – In a bowl, combine ground beef, breadcrumbs, garlic powder, Worcestershire sauce, and seasonings.
3. **Stuff eggs** – Form a meatloaf and place the hard-boiled eggs in the center.
4. **Bake** – Cook for 45 minutes, then slice and serve.

Eggnog

Ingredients:

- 4 large eggs
- 1 cup heavy cream
- 1 cup whole milk
- ½ cup sugar
- 1 tsp vanilla extract
- ½ tsp ground nutmeg
- ¼ tsp ground cinnamon

Instructions:

1. **Whisk eggs and sugar** – In a bowl, beat eggs with sugar until smooth.
2. **Heat milk and cream** – In a saucepan, bring milk and cream to a simmer.
3. **Combine** – Gradually add warm milk to egg mixture, then return to pan and cook until thickened.
4. **Chill** – Let cool, then refrigerate. Serve with a sprinkle of nutmeg.

Chocolate Lava Cake with Eggs

Ingredients:

- 4 oz semi-sweet chocolate
- ½ cup unsalted butter
- 2 large eggs
- 2 egg yolks
- ¼ cup sugar
- ¼ cup all-purpose flour
- Pinch of salt

Instructions:

1. **Preheat oven** – Set to 425°F (220°C) and grease ramekins.
2. **Melt chocolate and butter** – Heat in a bowl until smooth.
3. **Mix eggs and sugar** – Whisk eggs, egg yolks, and sugar, then combine with chocolate.
4. **Bake** – Spoon mixture into ramekins and bake for 12–14 minutes until edges are firm, but centers are soft.
5. **Serve** – Let cool for 1 minute, then invert onto plates.

Lemon Curd (Egg-Based)

Ingredients:

- 4 large egg yolks
- ¾ cup sugar
- ¼ cup lemon juice
- 2 tbsp lemon zest
- 6 tbsp unsalted butter

Instructions:

1. **Whisk yolks and sugar** – In a bowl, combine egg yolks and sugar.
2. **Cook curd** – In a saucepan, heat lemon juice and zest. Gradually whisk into egg mixture, cooking over low heat until thickened.
3. **Add butter** – Stir in butter until smooth.
4. **Cool** – Transfer to a jar and refrigerate.

Vanilla Custard

Ingredients:

- 2 large eggs
- 1 cup whole milk
- ½ cup sugar
- 1 tsp vanilla extract
- Pinch of salt

Instructions:

1. **Whisk eggs and sugar** – Beat eggs and sugar until smooth.
2. **Heat milk** – In a saucepan, bring milk to a simmer, then slowly pour into egg mixture.
3. **Cook custard** – Return to pan and cook over low heat, stirring until thickened.
4. **Cool** – Remove from heat, add vanilla, and let cool.

Tiramisu (Egg-Based Dessert)

Ingredients:

- 6 large egg yolks
- ¾ cup sugar
- 1 cup mascarpone cheese
- 1 cup heavy cream
- 1 cup strong coffee, cooled
- 2 tbsp rum (optional)
- 1 package ladyfingers
- Unsweetened cocoa powder for dusting

Instructions:

1. **Whisk egg yolks and sugar** – In a bowl, combine egg yolks and sugar until smooth.
2. **Mix mascarpone and cream** – Stir mascarpone into yolk mixture, then whip cream and fold in.
3. **Soak ladyfingers** – Dip ladyfingers in coffee and layer in a dish.
4. **Assemble** – Spread half of the mascarpone mixture over ladyfingers, then repeat layers.
5. **Chill** – Refrigerate for at least 4 hours, then dust with cocoa powder before serving.

Crème Brûlée

Ingredients:

- 4 large egg yolks
- 2 cups heavy cream
- ½ cup sugar
- 1 tsp vanilla extract
- ¼ cup sugar (for topping)

Instructions:

1. **Preheat oven** – Set to 325°F (160°C).
2. **Whisk yolks and sugar** – Beat yolks with sugar until smooth.
3. **Heat cream** – Bring cream to a simmer, then slowly add to egg mixture.
4. **Bake** – Pour into ramekins and bake in a water bath for 30–40 minutes until set.
5. **Caramelize** – Sprinkle sugar on top and use a kitchen torch to caramelize.

Meringue Cookies

Ingredients:

- 4 large egg whites
- 1 cup sugar
- ½ tsp vanilla extract
- ¼ tsp cream of tartar

Instructions:

1. **Preheat oven** – Set to 225°F (110°C) and line a baking sheet.
2. **Whip egg whites** – Beat egg whites with cream of tartar until soft peaks form.
3. **Add sugar** – Gradually add sugar, then whip until stiff peaks form.
4. **Shape cookies** – Spoon or pipe onto baking sheet.
5. **Bake** – Bake for 1.5–2 hours, then cool before serving.